Remember, students can get more pr
the sentences on pages 3–4, 7–8, 11–12, 14, and 17–18, as
described under "Sentence Practice."

Whose Verb List is Longer? To play this game, think of a noun (such
as *ball* or *dog*) then make a list of all the actions that the noun can
do. Compare the lists to see who has the most verbs, who has the
most creative verbs, etc.

Students can get additional practice finding verbs by using sentences
on pages 3–4, 7–8, 11–12, 14, and 17–18. After advanced students
find the verbs, ask them to identify the verb tense that is used or
rewrite the sentence and change the verb tense.

Proper That Whopper Two students list an equal number of common
nouns and trade lists. Next, they change the common nouns to
proper nouns by "naming" each noun. Inanimate objects can have
brand names or funny names (*Meet my pet pencil, Slim.*) This can be
a race.

All sentence pages may be used to check students' ability to
distinguish between proper nouns and common nouns. Have the
students write all nouns and circle proper nouns.

Link 'em Write nouns and words that describe them on separate
3 x 5 cards. Have students link the words together by supplying an
appropriate linking verb.

Pronoun Change Out Using noun cards from the previous activity,
ask students which pronoun they could use in place of the noun.
Explain that this is helpful when a noun is being used too many times
in a story.

You may also check students' ability to find pronouns by having them
circle pronouns on pages 7, 8, 11, 12, 17, and 18.

NOUNS

Everybody's talkin' about words
All the special kinds of words
Every word that you have heard
    and more

Learn how to use words
Write a story
Write a book
Everybody take a look

A noun is a special kind of word
    to me
It's anything that you can touch,
    hear, or see
Things are nouns, and it's true
That people and places are
    nouns, too

THINGS are nouns:

Everything that you can see
    is a noun
Everything that you can feel
    is a noun
Everything that you can hear
    is a noun
Everything that you can taste
    is a noun

Everything that you can smell
Everything is a noun!

PEOPLE are nouns:

Everybody that you know
    is a noun
Everybody that you don't know
    is a noun
People in your family
    are all nouns
People far from you and me
    Hey, everybody is a noun!

PLACES are nouns:

Everywhere that you have been
    is a noun
Every place that you have seen
    is a noun
Every planet, every star
    is a noun
This whole universe of ours
Every place, everywhere
    is a noun

Everybody's talkin'
    about words . . .

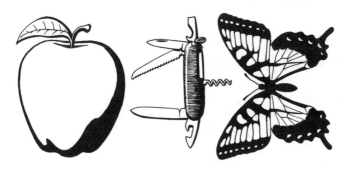

Things

People

Places

1. The dog ran.

2. The cat chased a mouse.

3. A bird flew over the house.

4. Bob saw a big red apple.

5. Mary and Joe went to a movie.

6. The author wrote a book about Japan.

7. Morgan rides a horse in the field.

8. Kito ate chicken and rice for dinner.

9. Ben filled the tub and took a bath.

10. Roy plays tag with Chang and Melvin.

11. Todd threw a ball to Isaac.

12. The teacher wrote sentences on the chalkboard.

13. Steven ate pizza with Holly and Maria.

14. The policeman walked down the street and opened a door.

15. The waiter brought the food quickly.

4

PROPER NOUNS

Proper nouns
Proper nouns
The big first letter
   whopper nouns
Because they give a noun
   a name
They have a capital letter

Washington, Baltimore,
Florida, China,
Mars, The Milky Way,
Katmandu, Rhode Island

These are certain places
They are proper nouns

If it's the name of a person
Or the name of a
   certain place
Or how about the name of
   a special thing?
The first letter better be
   uppercase
For a proper noun

Bob, Ralph, Mary,
Mr. Smith, Harry,
King of France,
Betty, Lance,
Mrs. Jones, and Larry

These are certain people
They are proper nouns

Capitalize the **proper**
No caps on the **common**. . .

White House is a proper noun.

PRONOUNS

I, me,
you, she,
her, him,
it, he,
they, them,
us, we

These words are pronouns

them

it

he

her

6

1. The fly landed on Bob.

2. Bob will fly to Mexico.

3. Veronica, Ralph, and Shelly built a fort, and they played in it.

4. The lifeguard whistles at us when we run.

5. The whistles at the store cost a quarter.

6. The principal waves to the students as they leave the school.

7. The waves of the ocean crash over the castle.

8. Grandma makes warm rolls for me.

9. Billy rolls down the mat, and Sasha turns a cartwheel.

10. The wind blew the kite into a tree.

11. I will wind the string around the yo-yo.

12. Jane and Juan will go with us in the car.

13. The band will play cool songs, and the fireworks will thrill the crowd.

14. The doctor is friendly, and she always smiles.

15. The teacher is fun because he teaches with music.

VERBS

Do VERB do VERB
Do VERB do VERB

Anything a noun can **do**
   is a verb

Do VERB do VERB
Do VERB do VERB

A verb is for doing
It's an action kind of word

When I **run**
When I **walk**
When I **move** around

I always **use** a verb
When I **write** it down

When I **talk**
When I **sing**, yeah
When I **dance**

I **use** a verb to **tell** you
I never **take** a chance

Do VERB do VERB
Do VERB do VERB . . .

*(Let's catch Eric
singing along!)*

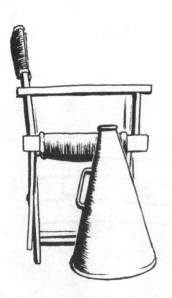

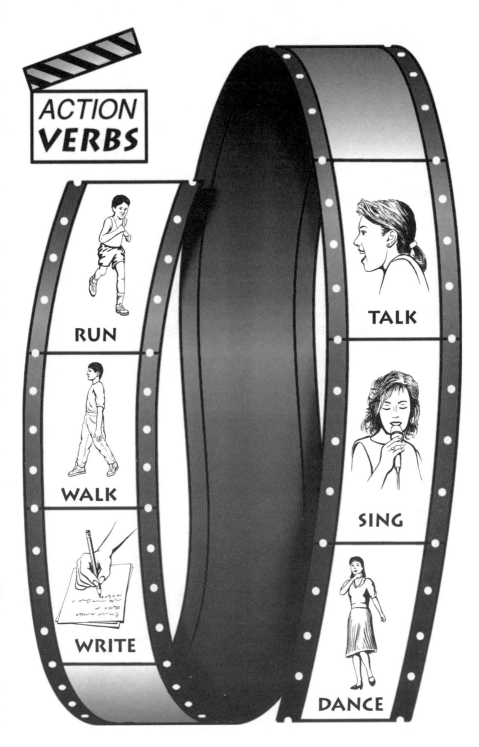

1. The children play.

2. The birds eat worms and sing in a tree.

3. The cars and trucks honk and beep when they sit on the highway.

4. Bees collect nectar and take it to the hive.

5. The frogs croak while the crickets chirp.

6. Barry and Maria draw and paint pictures of animals.

7. Brian beats the drums, Li strums the guitar, and Brad plays the bass.

8. The clock ticks and the hands move.

9. The chair squeaks when I sit in it.

10. The baby cries, eats, and sleeps.

11. The dog barked at the cat and chased it.

12. The owl hooted and screeched in the barn.

13. We saw a red light and stopped.

14. A family rode bicycles and walked in the park.

15. I planted a seed and a flower grew.

LINKING VERBS

Sometimes all a verb
   does is link two parts
   of a sentence together

This special kind of verb
   is called a linking verb

Here are a few
Let's learn them together

am, is, are, was, were,
   be, being, been
am, is, are, was, were,
   be, being, been

(repeat)

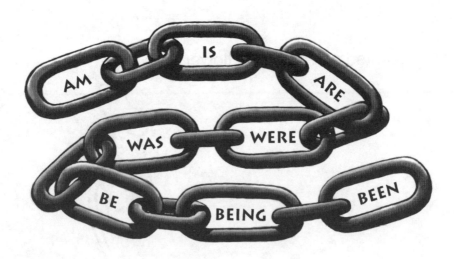

1. The folder is bright red.

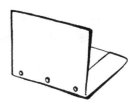

2. I am creative.

3. The bears were nice and cuddly.

4. The beds are lumpy.

5. The sunset was beautiful.

VERB TENSE

Earlier I **ran**
Now I **run**
Later I **will run** again

Yesterday I **swam**
Now I **swim**
Tomorrow I **will swim** again

Past, present, future
Everybody get the tense
Past, present, future
You will see it all makes sense...

	past	present	future
1.	walked	walk	will walk
2.	jumped	jump	will jump
3.	jogged	jog	will jog
4.	baked	bake	will bake
5.	fixed	fix	will fix
6.	rolled	roll	will roll
7.	turned	turn	will turn
8.	raked	rake	will rake
9.	chased	chase	will chase
10.	played	play	will play
11.	carried	carry	will carry
12.	shared	share	will share
13.	loved	love	will love
14.	skipped	skip	will skip
15.	went	go	will go
16.	sent	send	will send
17.	sang	sing	will sing
18.	sat	sit	will sit
19.	was	is	will be
20.	thought	think	will think

1. The barber cuts and dries hair.

2. The frog jumped off a log and swam in the pond.

3. Joanna will dance at the party.

4. The elephant was happy when he ate peanuts.

5. I swim in the pool when the weather is hot.

6. Ben went home and ate salad, spaghetti, and bread.

7. The lizard ran across the hot sand and sat under a rock.

8. We hung balloons from the ceiling after we baked a cake.

9. The fan blew papers off the desk, and I chased them down the stairs.

10. Michelle cut and pasted paper and made a swan.

11. Shawn read three books and wrote a report.

12. The team will practice hard, and they will win the game.

13. The actress smiled and waved at the fans.

14. Large pelicans dive in the water and catch fish.

15. Grandma and Grandpa fish at the lake.

ANSWERS

pages 3 and 4

<u>Nouns:</u> dog, cat, mouse, bird, house, Bob, apple, Mary, Joe, movie, author, book, Japan, Morgan, horse, field, Kito, chicken, rice, dinner, Ben, tub, bath, Roy, tag, Chang, Melvin, Todd, ball, Isaac, teacher, sentences, chalkboard, Steven, pizza, Holly, Maria, policeman, street, door, waiter, food

<u>Proper Nouns:</u> Bob, Mary, Joe, Japan, Morgan, Kito, Ben, Roy, Chang, Melvin, Todd, Isaac, Steven, Holly, Maria

<u>Verbs:</u> ran, chased, flew, saw, went, wrote, rides, ate, filled, took, plays, threw, wrote, ate, walked, opened, brought

pages 7 and 8

<u>Nouns:</u> fly, Bob, Bob, Mexico, Veronica, Ralph, Shelly, fort, lifeguard, whistles, store, quarter, principal, students, school, waves, ocean, castle, Grandma, rolls, Billy, mat, Sasha, cartwheel, wind, kite, tree, string, yo-yo, Jane, Juan, car, band, songs, fireworks, crowd, doctor, teacher, music

<u>Proper Nouns:</u> Bob, Bob, Mexico, Veronica, Ralph, Shelly, Grandma, Billy, Sasha, Jane, Juan

<u>Pronouns:</u> they, it, us, we, they, me, I, us, I, she, he

<u>Verbs:</u> landed, will fly, built, played, whistles, run, cost, waves, leave, crash, makes, rolls, turns, blew, will wind, will go, will play, will thrill, is, smiles, is, teaches

<u>Linking Verbs:</u> is, is

pages 11 and 12

<u>Nouns:</u> children, birds, worms, tree, cars, trucks, highway, bees, nectar, hive, frogs, crickets, Barry, Maria, pictures, animals, Brian,

drums, Li, guitar, Brad, bass, clock, hands, chair, baby, dog, cat, owl, barn, light, family, bicycles, park, seed, flower

Proper Nouns: Barry, Maria, Brian, Li, Brad

Pronouns: they, it, I, it, it, we, I

Verbs: play, eat, sing, honk, beep, sit, collect, take, croak, chirp, draw, paint, beats, strums, plays, ticks, move, squeaks, sit, cries, eats, sleeps, barked, chased, hooted, screeched, saw, stopped, rode, walked, planted, grew

page 14

Nouns: folder, bears, beds, sunset

Pronouns: I

Linking Verbs: is, am, were, are, was

pages 17 and 18

Nouns: barber, hair, frog, log, pond, Joanna, party, elephant, peanuts, pool, weather, Ben, home, salad, spaghetti, bread, lizard, sand, rock, balloons, ceiling, cake, fan, papers, desk, stairs, Michelle, paper, swan, Shawn, books, report, team, game, actress, fans, pelicans, water, fish, Grandma, Grandpa, lake

Proper Nouns: Joanna, Ben, Michelle, Shawn, Grandma, Grandpa

Pronouns: he, I, we, we, I, them, they

Verbs: cuts, dries, jumped, swam, will dance, was, ate, swim, is, went, ate, ran, sat, hung, baked, blew, chased, cut, pasted, made, read, wrote, will practice, will win, smiled, waved, dive, catch, fish

Linking Verbs: was, is

credits:

Male vocals: T. J. Rockenstein, Alan Bradley, and special guest appearance by D.J. Doc Roc.
Female Vocals: Jean July

Male spoken voice: Eric Leikam
Female spoken voice: Susan Rand

All instrumental performances by Brad Caudle.

Illustrations: Bart Harlan
Cover illustration: Anthony Guerra

Written and produced by Brad Caudle & Melissa Caudle.
Executive producer: Richard Caudle
© 1994 Brad Caudle & Richard Caudle

Page layout by Melissa Caudle and Richard Caudle.
Coordination of educational consultants: Kathie Caudle.

Recorded, mixed and mastered at Caudle Brothers Digital, Houston, Texas.

We dedicate this program to Tim Kelley and Tim Ackerman. Thank you for believing in Rock 'N Learn.

Meet Mr. Rock & Mr. Learn

Rock 'N Learn is actually two zany brothers—Brad and Richard Caudle—who decided that educational recordings for children could *and must* sound much better. So back in 1986, with only a $500 investment, they set out to revolutionize educational music with their first recording, *Multiplication Rock.* In the past decade, the Caudle Brothers have sold over 2.5 million tape and book programs, constantly revising their programs to get the most current sound possible. They also have produced a highly entertaining CD-ROM game and recently have begun creating the most wildly colorful videos on the planet. Richard holds masters degrees in both school psychology and business. Brad has a degree in electrical engineering and is an accomplished singer/musician who often appears in the local Houston music scene with various bands. When developing programs, the Caudle Brothers consult with skillful educators and feature the vocals of young, talented artists. Visit Rock 'N Learn's hot, new web site at www.rocknlearn.com.

"ROCK 'N READ™" SERIES

New educator-developed approach teaches reading skills by using familiar stories. Cassette includes slow version and fast version. Stories have a happy ending and a bonus rock song that teaches an important lesson about life.

RL966 Jack and the Beanstalk
RL967 The Three Little Pigs
RL968 The Ugly Duckling
RL969 The Little Red Hen

PHONICS BOX SET

Complete reading kit at an affordable price! Includes Phonics Deluxe I, Phonics Deluxe II, and Easy Readers below.
RL961

PHONICS DELUXE I

Short vowels, consonants, blends & more. Includes 50-minute tape and large 64-page reproducible activity book with puzzles, games, work sheets, and teaching tips. Ages 6 and up.
RL950

PHONICS DELUXE II

Long vowels, vowel combinations, "rule breakers," and more. Includes 50-minute tape and large 64-page reproducible activity book. Ages 6 and up.
RL951

PHONICS "EASY READERS"

Set of four readers following the format of Rock 'N Learn Phonics cassette programs. 12 stories provide sequentially-paced reading practice.
RL965

LETTER SOUNDS – PHONICS FOR BEGINNERS

The alphabet and sounds letters make, including consonant combinations. A 50-minute tape and "follow-along" book. Ages 4-7.

RL911

PHONICS VOLUME I & II

Covers material taught in Phonics Deluxe I & II above. Includes two cassettes and "follow-along" book. (Note: Does not include the activity pages.) Ages 6 and up.

RL900